Text copyright © 1999 Steve Turner
Illustrations copyright © 2001 David Mostyn
This edition copyright © 2001 Lion Publishing

The moral rights of the author and illustrator
have been asserted

Published by
Lion Publishing plc
Sandy Lane West, Oxford, England
www.lion-publishing.co.uk
ISBN 0 7459 4714 X

First edition 2001
10 9 8 7 6 5 4 3 2 1 0

A catalogue record for this book is available
from the British Library

Typeset in 16/22 Potrzebie
Printed and bound in Singapore

Dad...!

Steve Turner

Illustrations by David Mostyn

LION
Giftlines

Dad, You're Not Funny

A few of my mates
Come around to our place
And you're at the door
With a grin on your face.

You know that I know
You're a really good bloke
But I'll curl up and die
If you tell us a joke.

We don't want to hear
About your days at school
We don't want to watch
You try to be cool.

We don't want to know
How the world used to be
We don't want to see
Those videos of me.

We don't want to laugh
At your riddles and rhymes
At musty old tales
We've heard fifty times.

We don't want a quiz
Where we have to compete
We don't want to guess
Why the hen crossed the street.

So Dad, don't come in
Your jokes are so dated
I often pretend
That we're not related.

I'd pay you to hide
If I had my own money
The simple truth is –

Dad, you're not funny.

The Best Dad

My dad's
  much weaker than your dad
My dad's
  got less hair on his head

My dad
  snores louder than your dad
My dad
  spends more time in bed.

My dad's
  much weirder than your dad
My dad's
  got more flakes up his nose
My dad's
  less trendy than your dad
My dad
  wears more awful clothes.

My dad's

more sober than your dad

My dad's

got more wax in his ears

My dad

talks dafter than your dad

My dad

looks older by years.

My dad's

  got less teeth than your dad

My dad's

  got more sweat in his pits

My dad's

  much plumper than your dad

That's why I love him to bits.